Personal Application Workbook

for

The Way of Agape

by

Chuck and Nancy Missler

Koinonia House

The Way of Agape Workbook

© Copyright 1994, 1995, 1997, 1998, 1999,2000

Seventh Printing September 2000

Published by Koinonia House

PO Box D
Coeur d'Alene ID 83816-0347
ISBN 1-880532-57-3

All Scripture quotations are from the King James Version of the Holy Bible.

PRINTED IN THE UNITED STATES OF AMERICA

Table of Contents

Chapter 1: Introduction

The Way of Agape teaches you about a *new way* of loving. It's a way of loving that is totally opposite from the way the world teaches and is probably totally opposite from the way you have been used to, even as a Christian.

The Way of Agape is not just for women, nor is it just for married people. *Wherever there is a relationship, God's Way of Agape is needed.* It really doesn't matter if you have been a Christian seven months, seven years, or 77 years. It doesn't matter how many Scriptures you know, how many prayers you say, how many Bible studies you lead, or even how many books you write; it's still a moment-by-moment choice to "love God" and to lay your life down to Him so that His Love can be poured forth through you.

Purpose of the Workbook

The goal or purpose of this workbook is to stimulate you to apply the Scriptural principles presented in The Way of Agape textbook to your life. True spiritual growth comes not from simply reading a book or attending a Bible study, but by the personal application of the material to your life.

This workbook is designed to help you learn to *love God* so that He can then *love others* through you.

You will gain the maximum benefit from this workbook by reading a chapter in The Way of Agape textbook and then completing the corresponding chapter workbook questions. You will quickly see how specific Scriptures apply to your own situation. You will receive deeper insights into God's character and His great Love for you. You will also begin to understand your own *natural reactions* a little more clearly and, at the same time, learn an alternative way of dealing with them.

It is our desire to help you intimately experience God's Love, Wisdom, and Power in your daily life so you can have that "abundant life" He promises.

"I am come that they might have *life*, and that they might have it more abundantly." (John 10:10)

How To Use This Workbook

This *Personal Application Workbook* is designed to accompany The Way of Agape textbook. You should have your own textbook and your own workbook. Each chapter in the workbook corresponds to the same chapter in The Way of Agape textbook. The questions in the workbook should be completed *after* the corresponding chapter in the textbook has been read.

The workbook questions are divided into three categories: **Group Discussion Questions, Personal Questions**, and **Continue at Home Questions**.

- If you will be using this study for **personal Bible study**, it is suggested that you do all the workbook questions (Personal, Group, and At Home).

- If this study is to be used by **small discussion groups**, it is suggested that the leader of the group use the Group Discussion Questions and whatever Personal Questions are applicable. Continue at Home projects can be used during the week. (See the *Role of the Discussion Leader* at the end of this workbook.)

- Finally, if this study is to be used for a **large, corporate group** (where small discussion groups are not feasible), it is suggested that the appropriate questions be selected by the leadership and used for individual home study.

Personal Bible Study

Critical to any Bible study, whether it be personal or corporate, is prayer. Pray and ask God to search your heart and reveal anything that might hinder you from hearing Him. Then cleanse your heart of these things, so you can receive *all* that He has for you.

Along with your King James Bible, it is often helpful to have the following: a modern translation of the Bible (like the New American Standard Bible or the New International Version); a Bible Dictionary to look up any unfamiliar words, names and places; and a concordance (Strong's Concordance comes in a paperback form).

Read the appropriate chapter in the textbook. You must understand the principles and concepts of The Way of Agape textbook before you can really answer the questions properly and apply the principles to your life.

Look up all the Scriptures listed under each question. Meditate upon each one. It's the Word of God that will change your life, not a textbook or a class. Write out on 3x5 cards the Scriptures that particularly minister to you. Look up the important words in the original Hebrew or Greek, using your Strong's Concordance. Then you can be sure you are getting the *real* meaning of each word. So often the English translation in the Bible is far from what the original word meant.

Write out your answers in the space provided under each question. If you need more space, there are additional blank pages at the end of this workbook.

It's important to keep a personal journal. Write down all your experiences with God. Note the promises He gives you from Scripture, as well as the experiences He allows in your life. Express your real feelings and emotions about these things--no one should ever see your journal but you. Most importantly, write down the things that you give over to God as you cleanse your heart each day.

What a blessing and an encouragement this journal will be when you read it later on. In those times when you are going through a "valley," your entries in the journal will remind you of all that God has done for you and of His complete faithfulness to perform His promises. Your journal will give you the encouragement and the *hope* to make the same faith choices again.

Group Bible Study

This workbook, along with The Way of Agape textbook, can also be used for small group discussions. Learning takes place through the understanding and sharing of Biblical principles with intimate friends, such as in a small discussion group. A discussion group of about eight to ten people is ideal, and each of these groups should have a leader to guide the sharing. The *Role of the Discussion Leader* is explored in detail at the end of this workbook (Section Three).

The first thing to do in all Bible studies is to pray. Prayer is what changes things--our hearts, our attitude, our situation, other people, etc. Pray continually.

Always come to the study prepared, having first read the entire chapter in the textbook, then having completed the appropriate questions in the workbook.

Look up all the Scriptures listed under each question. Meditate upon each one. It's the Word of God that will change your life, not a textbook or a class. Write out on 3x5 cards the Scriptures that particularly ministered to you. Look up in your Strong's Concordance the important words in the original Hebrew or Greek. Then you can be confident of the true meaning of the words.

Be willing to join in the discussions. If you have completed the questions and have some understanding of the chapter, you will feel comfortable in sharing. The leader of the group is not there to lecture, but to encourage others to share what they have learned.

Have your answers applicable to the chapter in discussion. Keep the discussion centered upon the principles presented in The Way of Agape textbook, rather than on what you have "heard" others say or on what you have "read" elsewhere. Keep focused.

Be sensitive to the other members of the group. Listen when they speak and be encouraging to them. This will prompt more people to share.

Do not dominate the discussion. Participate, but remember that others need to have equal time.

If you are a discussion leader, suggested answers, additional suggestions, and helpful ideas are in the The Way of Agape Leader's Guide. Also, see the "Role of the Discussion Leader" section at the end of this workbook.

Above all, pray for God's guidance and grace to love Him as He desires and be that open vessel to pass along His Love.

*   *   *   *   *

"*Search the Scriptures*; for in them ye think ye have eternal life: and they are they which testify of Me." (John 5:39, emphasis added)

Chapter 2: Up in Flames

Overview

In order to show us His Love, God often has to "wound" us, as Hosea 6:1 says. But through that wounding, Scripture promises us, we *will* be healed. God uses our trials and tribulations not only to get our attention, but to stop us from going our own way. He purposely corners us to show us "*His more excellent way.*"

In the textbook, we don't learn techniques for appropriating God's Love. Only God is Love, and we can't learn to be what only God is. What we do learn, however, is *how to totally give ourselves over to God*, so that He, then, can love His Love through us. This is God's more excellent way.

The *Way of Agape* is: 1) learning what God's Love is and realizing that this is the same unconditional Love that He has for us; 2) learning how to lay our wills and our lives down to Him and love Him; and 3) learning that as we love Him, He will give us the Love and the ability to love others as ourselves.

God tells us that if we love in this way, *we shall live and have that abundant life that He has promised.* (Luke 10:28)

Group Discussion Questions

1. What is our *purpose* as Christians? (Romans 8:29; Ephesians 3:17-19; 1 Timothy 1:5; Ephesians 5:1-2; John 13:34-35; 1 John 4:16-17) How are we to fulfill this purpose? (Matthew 22:37-40; Mark 8:35; 1 John 3:16; 4:12)

2. Identify the specific actions and attitudes laid down by our Lord in Luke 14:25-35 for anyone who would be His disciple.

3. How would you describe "abundant Life?" (John 10:10)

4. Why do you think God allows trials in our lives? (Deuteronomy 30:19-20;13:3-4; Psalm 119:67; John 15:2)

5. 2 Corinthians 4:10 talks about the "dying of Jesus." Share what this means to you. What is the "life of Jesus" spoken about here?

6. Review in detail the three steps of God's *Way of Agape*. (Matthew 22:37-40; John 12:24-25; 2 Corinthians 4:10-12; Matthew 16:24)

7. 1 John 3:14 says that if we are not loving with God's Love, then we are dying. What does this mean to you?

Personal Questions

1. Have you or are you experiencing any situations or struggles similar to those that were shared in this chapter? If so, what situations?

2. READ Mark 10:17-22. Why do you think the rich young ruler could not give up his possessions? Can you name anything that would be difficult for you to give up now?

3. Summarize why it is so important to spend time alone with the Lord every day in order to live *The Way of Agape*?

4. How would you describe your own quiet time this week? List the things that seem to interfere.

5. 1 John 4:17 says: "... as He is, so are we in this world." Share what this means to you.

Continue at Home:

1. Write on a note card any Scriptures that particularly ministered to you in this chapter. Use them to help you apply these principles. Memorize them. Carry them with you or post them where you can see them as a reminder.

2. This week, talk to God about improving the quality of your daily quiet time. Schedule a specific time with Him. Listen to (and sing along with) taped worship songs for your praise time with God. Write out some of your prayers. Use a daily reading guide to help you be consistent with your Bible reading. Be accountable to someone for this time.

3. Ask God to show you the areas that you are still <u>not</u> willing to lay down to Him. (You might not even be aware of them.)

4. Begin a journal. Write down all the experiences God allows in your life this week that you need to "deal" with--situations you didn't handle properly or attitudes you developed that were not godly. Describe your own thoughts and emotions about the situation. *Confess* any of your thoughts or emotions that are not of faith and *repent* of them--choose to turn around from following them. *Give those negative thoughts and emotions to God,* and then *read His Word.* Ask Him to replace those negative things with His truth.

    MEMORIZE:
        John 12:24-25
        2 Corinthians 4:10-12
        Matthew 16:24

Chapter 3: What Is God's Love?

Overview

The definition for God's Love is found in 1 Corinthians 13:4-8. "Agape suffereth long, and is kind; Agape envieth not; Agape vaunteth not itself, is not puffed up, Doth not behave itself unseemly, seeketh not its own, is not easily provoked, thinketh no evil, Rejoiceth not in iniquity, but rejoiceth in the truth; Beareth all things, believeth all things, hopeth all things, endureth all things. Agape never faileth."

Have you ever tried to love like this? I did. For 20 years of my Christian walk, I thought to myself, "I am a Christian. I have God's Agape Love in my heart. All I need to do is use it." But somehow, it just didn't seem to work!

The truth is that none of us can love like 1 Corinthians 13. *Only God is Love, so only He can love like 1 Corinthians 13 perfectly.* (1 John 4:8) Our only responsibility is to choose to be an open vessel so God, who *is* Love, can love His Love through us.

Jesus Christ was the channel or the open vessel of God's Agape Love to us. He died so that God's Agape could be released through Him to us. This is exactly what God is asking each of us to do--be willing to surrender and yield our lives so His Agape (which is already in our hearts if we are born again) can be released through us to others.

"Verily, verily, I say unto you, Except a corn of wheat fall into the ground and die, it abideth alone: but if it die, it *bringeth forth much fruit.* He that loveth [hangs on to] his life shall lose it; and he that hateth [surrenders] his life in this world shall keep it unto life eternal." (John 12:24-25)

Group Discussion Questions

1. Define God's Love in your own words. List further qualities of God's Love found in the following passages: 1 Corinthians 13:1-8; 1 John 4:7-8, 16b; Galatians 5:22-24.

2. Name four other *characteristics* of God's Love spoken about in Chapter 3. (Luke 6:27-37; 2 Corinthians 3:17; 1 Corinthians 13:4-8) Expand on these passages.

3. Are we able, in our own power, to produce this kind of Love? Why or why not? (Romans 7:18; 1 John 4:16; John 15:5; 1 Corinthians 13:8)

4. Explain the difference between loving with God's Love and loving with human, natural love. (1 Corinthians 13:1-8; Luke 6:27-37; Galatians 5:22-24)

5. Describe the only requirement for having God's Love. (John 3:3-5; 17:26; Romans 5:5)

6. Define what further steps are required for us to love others with God's Love. (1 John 3:16; Matthew 16:24; 2 Corinthians 4:10-11)

7. 1 Corinthians 13:8 says that God's Love never fails. What does this mean to you? (Jeremiah 31:3; Psalm 89:33; 103:17)

8. Summarize the four *attributes* of God's Love that make it totally unique from any kind of human love. (See Supplemental Notes in Textbook.) Describe each attribute. (Ephesians 1:4-5; John 15:16; Jeremiah 31:3; Isaiah 63:9; Hosea 2:19-20; Deuteronomy 7:9)

9. What are the two sides of God's Love (called in the Hebrew, *chesed*)? (Psalms 103:4; Job 37:13; Romans 11:22)

10. Explain the difference between "taking a stand in God's Love" and "confronting" someone on your own. Can you give an example?

11. Before we "take a stand" in God's Love, what are some of the critical things *we* must remember to do? (Matthew 16:24)

12. God's Love often prompts a response from the one being loved. What are some responses you have noted? (Ephesians 5:13; Romans 2:4b; Jeremiah 31:3b)

Personal Questions

1. At this point, are you willing to lay down every facet of your life so that God can love others through you? If not, what areas are you still struggling with? (1 John 4:7-8,12,20)

2. What are some of your own negative thoughts and emotions that tend to block and prevent God's Love from flowing through you? What determines whether or not these things become sin in your life?

3. Can you give an example of a situation where you need to "take a stand in God's Love," but are having difficulty doing so?

4. Think of a situation where you *were able* to love with God's Love regardless of your feelings, the circumstances, or others' responses. Describe it.

5. Is there an area in your life right now where you can apply this teaching?

Continue at Home:

1. Write on a note card any Scriptures that particularly ministered to you in this chapter and use them to help you apply these principles. Memorize them.

2. Read over the <u>Agape Scriptures</u> in the Supplemental Notes section at the back of <u>The Way of Agape</u> textbook. Write on 3x5 cards the Scriptures that particularly help you and memorize them.

3. Spend quiet time this week recommitting every area of your life to God.

4. This week, pray and ask God to make you aware of your own negative and self-centered thoughts and feelings. In your journal, write down what God shows you. Choose to relinquish those thoughts to God. Confess you have "owned" (kept) them. Give those thoughts to God and then replace them with a few of your favorite Scriptures.

5. Ask God to fill you with His Love and allow that Love to be the motivation for all your choices each day.

READ:	MEMORIZE:
1 Corinthians 13	1 John 3:16
1 John 4	Galatians 5:22-24
Hosea 1-3	John 17:26

Chapter 4: Why Is God's Love So Important?

Overview

"Though I speak with the tongues of men and of angels, and have not Agape, I am become as sounding brass, or a tinkling cymbal. And though I have the gift of prophecy, and understand all mysteries and all knowledge; and though I have all faith, so that I could remove mountains, and have not Agape, *I am nothing*. And though I bestow all my goods to feed the poor, and though I give my body to be burned, and have not Agape, *it profiteth me nothing*." (1 Corinthians 13:1-3, emphasis added)

The reason God's Love is so critical, and the reason we are commanded to seek it with all our being, is because God is Agape. And having Agape (God) in our lives is the whole meaning and purpose for being called as a Christian. The Bible calls this "the end of the commandment" or the goal of our instruction. (1 Timothy 1:5)

Love is the reason we were created in the first place. And if we don't learn to love and be loved in the way God intended, we truly will have wasted our lives.

"He that loveth not, knoweth not God, for God is Love." (1 John 4:8)

Group Discussion Questions

1. In your own words summarize the reasons why God's Love is so important. (1 John 4:7-8; 1 Corinthians 13:2; 1 Timothy 1:5: John 13:34-35; Colossians 3:14)

2. Why do you think having and passing on God's Love should be the central issue of our lives? (1 Corinthians 13:1-3; Galatians 5:14; 1 John 3:14)

3. Galatians 5:14 tells us that God's Love is the "fulfillment of the law" (Galatians 5:14). What does this mean to you?

4. The Bible says having God's Love is the only way others will know we are Christians. (John 13:35) Why do you think this is so? Don't all Christians have God's Love showing through them?

5. John 15 tells us that having God's Love is proof we are abiding in Him. How is this so?

6. Explain what 1 Peter 4:8 means when it says God's Love "covers a multitude of sins."

Personal Questions

1. Is there an area in your life right now where you can apply this teaching?

2. Have you or are you now experiencing any situations or struggles similar to those that were shared in this teaching? If so, explain.

3. Does *loving with God's Love* have that first place in your life right now? (1 Peter 4:8) If not, why not?

4. Can others tell that you are a Christian by your Love? (1 John 4:8,12,20) How about your husband, your wife, your children, or your family?

5. Ephesians 3:19 tells us we are to be "filled with all the fulness of God." Have you ever experienced this? Share examples.

Continue at Home:

1. Write on a note card the Scriptures that particularly ministered to you in this chapter. Use them to help you apply these principles. Memorize them this week.

2. This week ask God to show you personally why His Love is so important to have and to pass on. In your journal, write the things God shows you. Be prepared to share.

READ:
  1 John 4
  1 Corinthians 13:1-3
  John 15
  Ephesians 3
  John 15 and John 17

MEMORIZE:
  1 Peter 4:8
  1 John 4:7-8,12,16-17
  1 Timothy 1:5
  John 13:34-35

Chapter 5: God's Love vs. Natural Love

Overview

God's Agape Love is totally opposite to human love. Human love is a self-centered love that is based upon our own understanding, our own circumstances, and others' responses. Everyone has human love; we are born with it. However, everyone *does not have* God's Love. God's Love is a gift we receive only when we ask Jesus Christ into our lives to be our personal Savior.

Agape is God's "supernatural" Love and it's the <u>only</u> solid basis upon which a relationship can be built. Only upon this foundation can all the human loves be built, rebuilt and allowed to grow.

One of the reasons why so many relationships are falling apart today is because God's Agape Love is missing. God's Love is missing because the people involved are either unbelievers or they have quenched God's Love in their hearts with bitterness, resentment, or unforgiveness and are not willing to give these things over to God.

"Because iniquity shall abound, the Agape of many shall wax cold." (Matthew 24:12)

Our responsibility as Christians is simply to learn *how* to be those open and cleansed vessels so that God's Agape Love already in our hearts--if we are believers--can easily and freely flow out into our lives.

Group Discussion Questions

1. Describe how God's Love differs from human love. (1 John 4:8; 1 Corinthians 13:4-8; Galatians 5:22-24; Romans 7:18)

2. Briefly define the three human loves: *storge, phileo,* and *eros.* Give an example of each.

3. Name four additional *characteristics* of human love described in this chapter.

4. Explain why human love is often referred to as a "need love."

5. What determines whether human love is good or bad? (1 Corinthians 3:11)

6. Summarize why it's so important to know the difference between God's Love and human love. (Matthew 24:12; Isaiah 59:2; 1 Corinthians 13:1-3; Song of Solomon 8:7)

7. Agape Love is "growing cold" in these end times. (Matthew 24:12) Why?

8. What should we do when we find we're not functioning on God's Love?

Personal Questions

1. Have you or are you now experiencing any situations or struggles similar to those that were shared in this chapter? If so, describe them.

2. Describe the kind of love you most often function on. Be honest.

3. Phileo love is the *result* of an _____ _____. However, with Agape, the _____ comes *first* and then the _____ follows. (John 15:13-15)

4. Has your love for God and others been dependent upon how you feel, what your circumstances are, and how the other person responds? Explain.

5. Using 1 Corinthians 12:31 and 1 Corinthians 13:1-4, 13, explain why loving God's Way is so important.

6. Is there an area in your life right now where you can apply this teaching? If so, where?

Continue at Home:

1. Write on a note card all the Scriptures that particularly ministered to you in this chapter. Use them to apply these principles. Memorize them.

2. Ask God to show you the times you begin to trust in your own ability to love (human love) rather than depending upon Him for His Love. Recognize these times and deal with your thoughts and emotions in the proper way. Be prepared to share examples.

3. This week, note in your journal the different types of human love you experience.

READ: MEMORIZE:
   1 Corinthians 13   Romans 7:18
   Romans 5   Isaiah 59:2
   Matthew 24   1 John 4:8
   1 John 4

Chapter 6: True Identity and Security

Overview

Our need *to be loved* can be fulfilled only by our knowing--without a doubt--that God loves us with an unconditional Love. We must know that His Love will never leave us or forsake us (Hebrews 13:5), no matter what we do or don't do. It's critical that we *know* that He loves us like this, not just in our heads but also in our daily lives.

No matter what our circumstances are as Christians, *we all need to live in the security of God's Love.* With this, we can do anything; without His Love, we are nothing. God's Love is the only basis and the only foundation upon which we can build our lives.

Knowing God loves us is the only thing that will give us our *identity* and our *security* in this life. Love and identity are often considered synonyms.

Our security and identity do not come from the conditional loves of others, from our accomplishments, or from our circumstances, but only from knowing that God loves us unconditionally and personally.

We need to hear and *know* Isaiah 43:3-4 over and over again, "I am the Lord...[you are] precious in my sight...and I love you [have loved you]."

Group Discussion Questions

1. Man has two basic needs. Define them and explain how they can be fulfilled. (1 Corinthians 13:2c; Jeremiah 31:3; 1 John 3:14; 4:12)

2. Consider if these two needs can ever be permanently met by others, things, or accomplishments. (Philippians 4:19; 1 Corinthians 3:11; Psalm 73:25) Share your thoughts.

3. If God's Love *has become* our total identity and security, what happens to us when we stumble and fall? What happens to us if His Love *is not* our complete security?

4. When we sin and do something that causes God's Spirit to be quenched in us, what happens to God's Love in our hearts? (Matthew 24:12; Ephesians 4:30a; 1 John 1:9)

Personal Questions

1. Our need *to be loved* brings us our_____ and our _____. (Isaiah 49:16; 54:10; Hebrews 13:5) Our need *to love* brings us our _____ and our _____. (1 Timothy 1:5; Philippians 1:21; 1 John 4:12) Give personal examples of each.

2. On what do you depend for your identity and security? Give examples. What happens when these things change or let you down?

3. Summarize what you tend to rely upon to fulfill your need for meaning and purpose. Do these things ever disappoint you?

4. Using 1 Corinthians 12:31 with 1 Corinthians 13:1-4,13, explain why we have the need to *to be loved*.

5. READ John 14:15-21,23 and John 15:1-10. Briefly describe why we also need *to love*. (Galatians 5:14)

6. Is there an area in your life right now where you can apply this teaching? If so, what area?

Continue at Home:

1. On a note card, write out the Scriptures that particularly ministered to you in this chapter. Use them to help you apply these principles. Memorize them.

2. Every day this week, make a special time to be with the Lord. Choose to give Him all your expectations, desires, and emotional needs. Ask Him to meet these needs and give you His Life. Once you are a cleansed vessel, ask Him to help you put the interests of others (your spouse, family, etc.) above your own.

3. Write out on 3x5 note cards the Who I Am in Christ Scriptures from the Supplemental Notes in the back of the textbook. Pick the ones that particularly minister to you and memorize them.

READ:
    Isaiah 43
    Philippians 1
    Psalm 18

MEMORIZE:
    John 15:16
    Ephesians 1:4
    Galatians 2:20
    Colossians 1:21
    Philippians 1:21

Chapter 7: Knowing God Loves Us

Overview

Before we can go any further in God's Way of Agape, we need to know without a doubt that we are loved by the Father; that He has laid down His Life expressly to give us His Love through Jesus Christ; and that He has called and elected us to be His vessels of Love.

1 John 3:16 states: "Hereby we *know* [have living experience] He loves us, because He laid down His Life for us."

If we know these things, we will have the confidence and the trust to lay our wills and our lives down to Him and love Him in return.

Many of us do not realize that when we *don't* lay our lives down to Him, and we hang on to our resentment, pride, bitterness, doubt, fear, anger, unforgiveness, insecurity, self-pity, worry, anxiety and irritability, we quench God's Love in our hearts. These negative emotions not only hamper our ability to love others, but they also prevent God's Love from coming forth into our own lives and showing us how much He loves us personally.

Experiencing God's Love in our own lives is the only thing that will allow us to intimately know Him. Experiencing His Love in our lives is also the only thing that will give us that consistent hope for the future--hope which leads us to faith and the ability to trust God in everything, even though we can't see or understand where He is leading us.

Group Discussion Questions

1. Share why *knowing God loves us* is the first step in living God's Way of Agape. (1 Corinthians 3:11; 1 John 4:19; Hebrews 13:5; 2 Timothy 1:12b)

2. Describe several ways that we can *know* God loves us. (Jeremiah 31:3; 1 John 4:10; John 3:16; Romans 5:5; 8:16; John 10:10)

3. How does God communicate His Love to us? (Psalm 119:159-160; 1 John 3:16; Isaiah 43:1-4) Give examples.

4. Knowing God loves us gives us *hope* for the future. Why? (Jeremiah 29:11; 1 John 3:2; Hebrews 6:19)

Personal Questions

1. Are you experiencing a daily, personal, and intimate relationship with God? Do you *know* His Love? (Ephesians 3:17-19; Psalm 86:5-7; 27:5,13) If not, ask God what is blocking you from knowing Him and experiencing His Love. (Be sure to note the things He shows you this week.)

2. Are you aware of any negative thoughts and emotions that are preventing you from experiencing God's Love?

3. Summarize why is it so critical to give these negative thoughts over to God. (Isaiah 59:2; Matthew 16:24-25; 2 Corinthians 4:10-11; Philippians 1:20-21) How does knowing that God loves you help you to lay these things aside? (Psalms 37:23-24)

4. What key points in this chapter are you still struggling with or having difficulty with?

5. If we really knew how much God loves us, we would never _____ what God would allow in our lives. (Isaiah 43:1-4; Matthew 10:29-31; 2 Timothy 1:7) Are there any situations in your life right now that are causing you to fear? How does *knowing that God loves you personally* change your attitude about these situations?

6. Is there an area in your life right now where you can apply this teaching? If so, what area?

Continue at Home:

1. Write on a note card the Scriptures that particularly ministered to you in this chapter. Use them to help you apply these principles. Memorize them.

2. Over the next week, ask God to enable you to experience His love in a new way. Be sure your heart and life are cleansed.

3. Write out the Scriptures from the Knowing God Loves Me chart in the Supplemental Notes at the back of the textbook. Write them on 3x5 cards and put your own name before each of the verses. As you read the Scriptures aloud, choose to believe what God is saying to you personally.

READ:
    1 John 3
    John 14 and 15
    Psalm 18
    Isaiah 43
    Ephesians 3:14-21

MEMORIZE:
    1 John 4:10
    Isaiah 43:1b-2,5
    Hebrews 13:5
    John 17:26
    Jeremiah 29:11

Chapter 8: What Does It Mean to Love God?

Overview

What exactly does it mean to love God? God's Word tells us very clearly--loving God is keeping His commands. We don't have to worry about which specific commands to keep as they are all summed up in one: "Love the Lord thy God, with all thy heart, and with all thy soul, and with all thy mind." And, "Love thy neighbor as thyself." (Matthew 22:36-40)

When we walk in obedience to these two commandments, we will be loving God as He desires. These two commandments are inseparable and must go in the order they were given. In other words, we can't love others as ourselves until we have *first* loved God with all our heart, mind and soul. We must first learn to love God--become that open vessel--so God, then, can love others through us.

The verb that is used for love in these two commandments is "agapao." To agapao God means to continually seek to obey, trust, and follow God's Will and not our own. In other words, we are to continually yield our own thoughts, emotions, and desires that are contrary to His and choose to worship and serve Him only.

Loving God is not an emotional feeling. It's not an emotional high. *Loving God is losing self to the point where we can say, "there was not a 'me' (self) there,"* only God. This is the point where we will know Jesus is not just *in* our lives, *He is our Life.*

Group Discussion Questions:

1. Define the Greek word *agapao* (to love). (John 12:24; Ephesians 5:2b; Luke 9:23) How does *agapao* differ from *storge* or *phileo* love?

2. Describe the difference between the verb *agapao* that we are studying here and the noun *Agape* that we studied in Chapter Three. (1 John 4:8b)

3. God commands us to love Him with all our heart, will, and soul. Summarize what this means to you. (Matthew 16:24; 2 Corinthians 4:10-11; John 12:24-25; Philippians 1:21)

4. Is our ability to love God dependent upon our feelings, circumstances, or other's responses? Why/Why not? Give examples.

5. Can we *agapao* bad things? Give some contemporary examples. (Matthew 22:37-39; John 3:19; 12:43; Luke 6:32)

6. To love God means to lose self. (John 12:24-25) What exactly does "self" mean in this context?

7. Summarize the three steps of loving God. (Matthew 4:1-10; Philippians 2:8; Luke 22:42; Luke 14:26-27; 2 Corinthians 4:11; Luke 5:11; Romans 12:1)

8. Explain what it means *to become one* with God. (1 John 4:17; Philippians 1:21; Galatians 2:20) How does this happen?

9. We can't serve God with our words alone. What must we also put alongside? (2 Corinthians 8:11; 2 Timothy 3:5) Give examples.

10. Define *truth*. (John 6:63; Matthew 3:16-17) Why is Jesus called the Truth? (John 1:1,4; 14:6; Jeremiah 1:12; Ezekiel 12:25)

Personal Questions

1. Describe some of the things in your own life that you *agapao*. Be specific.

2. READ: Matthew 16:24. Write out this verse and memorize it. What are the three steps of loving God mentioned here?

3. What must <u>we</u> do before God's Love can be manifested through us to others? (John 12:24; 15:3-4; Luke 14:26; Ephesians 5:2; 1 John 3:16)

4. In your own life, what are some of the negative thoughts, emotions, and desires that are the most difficult for you to deny or bar yourself from following? What happens when you give in to these thoughts and feelings and choose to follow them?

5. Are there areas in your life right now where you are having difficulty trusting God because of your feelings, your situation or another person's responses? Explain.

6. Do you love (agapao) God enough that you are willing to die to your own justified hurts, fears and doubts, etc., so that His Life can come forth through you? (John 21:15-17; Matthew 10:37-39; Luke 14:26-27) Yes/No? Express your feelings.

7. Are there any key points in this chapter that you are still struggling with or having difficulty with?

8. Are there any other areas in your life where you may be able to apply this teaching?

Continue at Home:

1. Write on a note card the Scriptures that particularly ministered to you in this chapter. Use them to help you apply these principles. Memorize them.

2. Over the next week, ask God to show you the areas where you are not loving Him. Write down in your journal what He shows you. Ask Him to help you the next time these areas come up to choose to obey Him, trust Him, and follow Him, rather than give in to your "old ways."

3. The reality of denying ourselves is a painful and difficult task. It is impossible to accomplish apart from Christ working in us. Our responsibility is only to be willing--willing to continually yield ourselves to Christ and allow Him to do the job through us. Ask God to continually reveal your own willingness (or unwillingness) to "die to self." Note what He shows you in your journal.

4. Recognize this week some of the "results" of your loving God. (Galatians 5:22-23; Ephesians 3:16-17; Romans 8:28; John 13:35) Ask God to show you more ways you can *agapao* your husband, your wife, your children, your family, your friends, your co-workers and your neighbors.

READ:
  Hosea 1-3
  John 14
  1 John 4
  Philippians 2:5-11

MEMORIZE:
  John 12:24-26
  John 14:21,23
  Philippians 2:7-8
  Luke 22:42
  Galatians 2:20
  Matthew 10:39

Chapter 9: Satan's Three Temptations

Overview

Satan tries everything he can to keep us from loving God--to keep us from giving ourselves completely over to God and putting Him first in our lives. If Satan can do this, he stops God's Love not only from being experienced in our lives, but also from being passed on to others. That's Satan's stated goal.

Satan is after our faith itself. If he can just plant a seed of doubt and unbelief in us towards God, he has won--because it constantly takes faith to love God.

Satan will do everything he can to keep us from obeying, trusting and following God--from laying our wills and our lives down to Him moment by moment. We must always remember "greater is He That is in us [meaning Jesus], than he that is in the world [meaning Satan]" (1 John 4:4).

Jesus gave us a victorious example to follow. The Bible tells us He was tempted in all areas just as we are (Hebrews 2:18). In Matthew 4:1-10 Jesus gives us the proper rebuttals to *all* of Satan's accusations and He tells us exactly how to love God instead.

God has all the Love we need; He has all the Wisdom we need; and He has all the Power we need. We simply must be willing to make those proper *faith choices*--those Jesus has laid out for us--and God will do the rest.

"Blessed is the man that endureth temptation: for when he is tried, he shall receive the crown of life, which the Lord hath promised to them that love Him." (James 1:12)

Group Discussion Questions

1. Why is Satan so intent upon keeping us from experiencing "abundant life?" (Ephesians 3:19; Romans 8:2-6)

2. Satan does not want us to love God. Summarize the three temptations he constantly throws at us.

3. Why does God allow these temptations in our lives? (Deuteronomy 8:2; 30:19; 13:3-4)

4. How does Jesus' refusal of Satan's temptations illustrate John 12:23-26 and 2 Corinthians 4:11-12?

5. Jesus resisted Satan and was obedient through the power of God's Word. According to James 1:21-25, how is God's Word to work in our lives?

Personal Questions

1. READ: Matthew 4:1-10. Write out Satan's three temptations and translate them into your own words.

Matthew 4:1-4

Matthew 4:5-8

Matthew 4:8-10

2. As you look at your own life, can you see any examples of Satan's three temptations?

3. From Matthew 4:1-10, write out Jesus' rebuttals to Satan's temptations. Memorize them. (See Deuteronomy 8:17; 6:16; Exodus 17:7 for explanation of second temptation.)

Continue at Home:

1. Write down the Scriptures that particularly ministered to you in this chapter. Use them to help you apply these principles. Memorize them.

2. Write out James 1:12-15. Summarize what James is saying.

3. Watch this week for Satan's temptations. Note them and choose, instead, to love God.

READ:
  James 1
  Deuteronomy 8
  Deuteronomy 30:15-20

Chapter 10: "Ye Are the Temple of God"

Overview

God is a God of meticulous detail and precision. When He says "love Me with all your *heart* (kardia)," He means something very specific. When He says "love Me with all your *willpower* (dianoya)," He means something else. And when He says "love Me with all your *soul* (psyche)," He again means something totally different. Therefore, in order to love God as He desires, we must first understand exactly what our heart, willpower, and soul are. Then we will be able to totally give ourselves over to Him as He commands.

God often uses word pictures or analogies in the Bible to help us understand a little more clearly what He is saying. One of these word pictures is 1 Corinthians 3:16 and it's very applicable in this context. "Know ye not that ye are the temple of God, and that the Spirit of God dwelleth in you?"

Paul, I believe, is making an analogy here by saying that our bodies are now the dwelling place of the Holy Spirit. He is saying that there is a mystical correlation between the physical Temple of God in the Old Testament and our bodies that are now the temple of God. I believe the Holy Spirit is telling us that the physical Temple in the Old Testament, where He used to dwell, is a model or a blueprint of a New Testament believer where God dwells now.

"For ye are the temple of the living God; as God hath said, I will dwell in them, and walk in them; and I will be their God, and they shall be My people." (2 Corinthians 6:16)

Thus, in order to understand ourselves better, in The Way of Agape textbook we compare our bodies to the actual layout and structure of Solomon's Temple. And by so doing, we gain a better insight into what exactly our spirit, our heart, our will, and our soul are. Then we will be able to go on and love (agapao) God with each of these areas in the way He desires.

Group Discussion Questions: (Choose the most appropriate questions)

1. What is the purpose of comparing Solomon's Temple with our bodies? Does seeing the Temple of God graphically enable you to love God more? (1 Corinthians 6:19-20; 3:16; 1 Kings 8:10-11) Why do we use Solomon's Temple as a model of the New Testament believer? Why not use Herod's or Nehemiah's Temple? (1 Chronicles 28:11-12,19-20)

2. Do you think the Temple model is useful in identifying our heart, will and soul? (Hosea 12:10)

3. Share the reasons why you think we so desperately need to be born again. (Romans 1:21-25; 3:11-12; John 3:3,5) What are some of the things we receive as a result of being born again? (Ezekiel 36:26; John 14:23; Colossians 1:27)

4. What is God's purpose for the new Life He has placed in our hearts? (Ephesians 5:17-18; John 4:14; 7:38)

5. Define the *new Spirit* we receive as a result of being born again. (John 6:63; Job 33:4)

6. Describe the *new heart* we receive as a result of being born again. (Ezekiel 36:25-27; 1 Peter 3:4; Romans 5:5; Colossians 1:27; 1 John 5:11-12) What was our heart life like *before* we were born again? (Jeremiah 17:9; Isaiah 47:10d; Genesis 8:21d; Mark 7:21)

7. What is the primary difference between our <u>old</u> heart and our <u>new</u> heart? (Romans 3:11-12; Colossians 3:9-10; 2 Corinthians 5:17)

8. With this in mind, can we have real and lasting life change *before* we are born again? Why/Why not? (Jeremiah 17:9) Do you have any personal examples?

9. Our new "heart life" is God's supernatural Life. Describe what this is. (Romans 5:5; Hebrews 8:10; Galatians 4:6) If the only life that now exists in our hearts is God's Life, what part of us still needs constant transformation? (Romans 12:1-2; 1 Corinthians 6:20; 2 Corinthians 4:16)

10. How does understanding our brand-new heart life help us make better choices?

11. Describe what our new willpower is and why it is it such a *critical* area. (Deuteronomy 30:19-10; Hebrews 8:10-11) What are the two parts of our willpower? (Philippians 2:13) What do the two bronze pillars on the porch symbolize? (Deuteronomy 30:19; Matthew 26:39; Philippians 2:13)

12. Describe our soul. What is its function? (1 Corinthians 6:20; Ephesians 5:17-18; 2 Corinthians 4:10) What's the difference between "heart life" and "soul life"? (Proverbs 4:23; Isaiah 58:10-11)

13. Our souls are a neutral area that can either be filled with God's Life or self life. What is it that determines which life will be expressed? (Isaiah 59:2; James 1:21-22)

14. If, as born-again believers, we have God's Life in our hearts, where does our "self life" come from? (Proverbs 5:22; John 8:34; Romans 6:16)

15. Colossians 3:8-10 tells us we are to "put off" the old man and "put on" the new. What exactly does this mean? (Ephesians 4:22-24; Romans 6:11-13) Scripturally, what is this *process* called?

16. When we were born again, we received a brand-new spirit, a brand-new heart and a brand-new will. What parts of our body, then, are not yet regenerated, but are in the process of santification?

17. Describe what "walking after the flesh" means. (Galatians 5:17-21) What does "walking after the spirit" mean? (Galatians 5:22-25) Give examples.

18. Define the "power of sin." (Romans 7:20-21,23) Where does the power of sin dwell? (Romans 7:23) What is its purpose? (Colossians 3:10; Philippians 3:14; Romans 8:29) Who is the author of the power of sin? (Isaiah 14:12-15) What areas does God allow the power of sin to access?

19. Since our old heart (the old man) no longer exists (Romans 6:6) and sin's hold on us is broken (Romans 6:7-14,22), where is the battle now fought between the power of God and the power of sin? (Romans 7:21-25; 6:13)

20. According to the Temple model, what is our body and what is its purpose? (Philippians 1:20; 1 Corinthians 6:19-20)

Personal Questions:

1. For each part of Solomon's Temple listed below, name the corresponding part in the born-again believer:

Holy of Holies = _____   Inner Court = _____

Holy Place = _____   Outer Court = _____

Porch = _____   Hidden Chambers = _____

2. Do these Temple charts help you to understand yourself better? Explain.

3. Ephesians 5:17-18 tells us what God's Will is for us. Explain what is it and how we accomplish it in our lives. (Matthew 22:37; John 12:24; Luke 9:23)

4. Which Temple chart most appropriately describes you the majority of the time? When do you tend to be *singleminded*? *Doubleminded*? Give examples.

5. If you see yourself in **Chart 6,** name some of the things that you know blocks God's Life in your heart.

6. Did you ever try to change or "improve" yourself before you were born again? If so, what happened?

7. Have you ever personally experienced God's Love flowing through you to another person when you knew you had none of your own to give? How about God's Wisdom? His Power?

8. Are there any key points in this chapter that you are still struggling with or having difficulty with?

Continue at Home:

1. Write on a note card all the Scriptures that ministered to you in this chapter. Use them to help you apply these principles. Memorize them.

2. Go over the charts in this chapter every day. Become familiar with them. At the end of the week, take a piece of paper and, as best as you can, draw **Chart 5** and **Chart 6** without looking. Then define in your own words what heart, will, and soul are. Know the differences between each.

3. Conduct an experiment: Watch for incidents in your life this week where you experience being **Chart 5**--singleminded, showing forth God, and walking after His Spirit. Also note this week the times you are **Chart 6**. When you recognize this, stop, pray, identify the problem, confess it, repent of it, give it to God, and get into His Word. Be prepared to share the results of your experiment.

    MEMORIZE:
        Ezekiel 36:26
        Philippians 2:13
        Romans 6:6-7
        Ephesians 5:17-18
        1 Corinthians 6:20

Chapter 11: Loving God With All Our Heart

Overview

The reason it's important for us to learn how to love God with all our heart, is that our *heart life* is the center core or the true essence of our whole person. Our heart is the place where all our thoughts, emotions, and desires originate--it's the foundation upon which everything else is built and all continuing activity depends.

When we accept Christ as our savior, He comes into our hearts bringing His Love and Life with Him. As long as we make the appropriate faith choices, our hearts will remain open and we will continue to do God's Will from our hearts--loving Him with all our hearts. However, when we say "no" to God's voice because we are hurting, angry, fearful, unforgiving or resentful, God's Spirit in our hearts becomes quenched and His Love is not able to flow.

"Doth a fountain send forth at the same place sweet water and bitter?" (James 3:11) "My brethren, these things ought not so to be." (verse 10)

God's Life in our hearts is often spoken of in the Bible as a "fountain of living water" that wells up within us, gushes forth, and fills us to overflowing. God desires that His fountain of living water in our hearts might freely flow through us to all we come in contact with.

Therefore, we not only love God with all our heart at our new birth-- when we become one heart with Him--we also love God with all our heart every time we allow His Life in our hearts to be the motivation for all we choose to do.

Group Discussion Questions:

1. Describe how we become *one heart* with God. (1 John 3:3-5; Ezekiel 11:19; Jeremiah 32:39; 1 John 5:12)

2. Loving God with all our heart means allowing God's Life in our heart to be the *motivation* for all we choose to do. Explain what this means. (Ephesians 6:6c; Romans 6:17b; 2 Corinthians 5:14a) Can you give some examples?

3. Describe our heart and explain why it's such an important area. (Matthew 7:24-25; Proverbs 4:23b; 14:30a; Matthew 7:24-25)

4. What's the *purpose* for God's supernatural Life in our hearts? (Ephesians 5:17-18; John 7:38; John 4:14) What must occur *in us* for God's Life to come forth? (Romans 6:11-13) What happens if we choose not to do this? (Psalm 119:70a; Hebrews 3:13; Matthew 13:15). Give examples.

5. Define sin. (Isaiah 59:2; Romans 14:23c; 1 John 5:17a)

6. Name some common sins we don't often recognize. What happens to God's Love when we sin?

7. Are all negative thoughts sin? Why/Why not? When do they become sin?

8. Define pride. (Isaiah 14:13-14; 47:8)

9. In James 3:10-12, it describes the "pure water coming out bitter." What does this mean and why does this grieve God? (James 3:10b)

10. Name the four types of hearts described in Luke 8:11-15. Briefly describe each one.

11. How does understanding our brand-new heart help us in making godly choices?

12. In review, loving God with all our heart means essentially two things. What are they? (Ezekiel 36:26; 1 John 5:12; Ephesians 6:6c; 2 Corinthians 5:14)

Personal Questions:

1. Have you or are you experiencing any situations or struggles similar to those that were shared in this teaching? If so, what situations?

2. Which of the following tend to motivate your choices and actions? (circle those that apply to you)

fear	hurt	doubt	anger
anxiety	guilt	pride	bitterness
resentment	insecurities	negative thoughts	
defensiveness	need to control	other_____	

3. What happens when you choose to follow these thoughts? Next time this occurs, what Scriptures could you use to replace them?

4. 1 Peter 4:2 tells us, we "no longer should live the rest of [our lives] to the lusts of men but to the _____ __ _____."

5. How can we know what the Will of God is? (Psalms 32:8; 119:9,105,130,169)

6. When you must make a decision and you're not certain of God's Will, what are the four things you should do?

7. Are there any key points in this chapter that you are still struggling with or having difficulty with?

Continue at Home:

1. Write on a note card all the Scriptures that particularly ministered to you in this chapter. Use them to help you apply these principles. Memorize them.

2. Become aware of the negative thoughts that take away your peace. Note them in your journal. Confess them, repent of them, and then give them to God. Don't let them accumulate and separate you from God.

3. Watch over your heart, as Scripture tells us, and let His Life in your heart be the *motivation* for all you choose to do this week.

4. Ask God to help you recognize and deal with those "subtle sins" you often commit without even realizing it.

5. Continue your exercise of seeing how long you can stay as **Chart 5** (singleminded). When you slip and become **Chart 6**, how long does it take you to "clean up" and return to being **Chart 5**?

> READ:
>> John 3
>> Galatians 5
>> Romans 6 and 7
>> James 3

Chapter 12: Loving God With All Our Willpower

Overview

We love God with all our willpower when we choose to trust His Spirit to perform in our lives and not our own ability and power.

We have a constant choice as to whom we will "yield our members." We can make an "emotional choice" and give in to our own thoughts and feelings and do our own will, or we can make a "faith choice" and trust God in spite of our feelings and circumstances, and rely upon Him to accomplish His Will in our lives.

Our constant choice is the *key* to our Christian walk. It's our faith choices that allow God's Life to come forth from our hearts, permeate our being and love others through us, regardless of how we feel. Born-again believers are the only ones who have this free choice decision, because we are the only ones who have a supernatural power within us to perform something different than what we think, feel, or want to do!

God always has Love for that other person. Our only responsibility is to choose to be that open and cleansed vessel so He can love that other person through us.

Group Discussion Questions: (Choose the most appropriate questions)

1. When we are born again, we receive a brand-new spirit and a brand-new heart. What else do we receive? (Hebrews 8:10; 10:16 *Be sure to check the Greek)

2. More precisely translated, what does the word mind (*dianoia*) in the First Commandment mean? (Matthew 22:37)

3. Why didn't God command the Old Testament saints to love Him with all their wills? (Deuteronomy 6:5; Galatians 4:6; 1 Corinthians 6:17)

4. In this chapter we use the term "supernatural willpower." Summarize what this means. (Matthew 26:39d, 1 Peter 4:2; 1 Corinthians 7:37) Why are Christians the only ones who possess this supernatural willpower? (Romans 7:18)

5. Describe the purpose of our willpower. (1 John 5:20; Ephesians 1:18-19-- again, see Greek) What are the two parts of our willpower? (Philippians 2:13; Deuteronomy 30:19-20)

6. Define what is meant by *free choice*. (John 10:17-18) Do all people have free choice? Why/Why not? (Ephesians 2:2-3; 4:17-19; Colossians 1:21)

7. Why is our willpower so critical? (Jeremiah 21:8; Ephesians 1:18; 1 John 5:20--see Greek)

8. Explain why our willpower is often described as "the keys to the kingdom." (Matthew 16:19; Isaiah 22:22; Revelation 3:7)

9. When we make a *faith choice*, can we know it was genuine by how we feel? Why/Why not? Describe some faith choices you have made in your life.

10. If we make the right faith choices, what happens to our *feelings* and our uncontrolled emotions? (Mark 9:24) Are we responsible to change our feelings? Who is? What is our responsibility? (Isaiah 1:19; Matthew 26:39; Luke 5:5)

11. When we make faith choices, whose life is lived in our soul? Why is this called *singlemindedness*? Explain.

12. Scripture tells us that when we make *faith choices,* we are freed from sin. How does this work? (Romans 6:6-7; Galatians 5:24; John 14:30c) What else occurs? (Zechariah 4:6c; Luke 1:45)

13. What three things happen when we choose to follow our <u>own</u> thoughts, emotions and desires over what God is prompting us to do? (Luke 8:14; Romans 7:15,19,23; James 1:8; Proverbs 5:22; John 8:34; Isaiah 59:2) Give examples.

14. Why is Satan thrilled when we make emotional choices? (Joel 1:10,12; Luke 11:17; Jeremiah 7:28; Luke 8:14) Why is this called *doublemindedness*? (James 1:8)

15. Where does sin begin? (James 1:14-15; 4:17; Romans 14:23) What is the consequence of allowing sin to proceed? (Ephesians 4:19; 1 Corinthians 5:6-7; Lamentations 3:44; Galatians 5:19-21)

16. READ: 2 Samuel 11:2-4. From this story about David, at what stage did he commit sin? At that point, could he have stopped it?

17. Contrast *walking after the Spirit;* **Chart 5** (Galatians 5:24-25; Romans 8:13; Luke 11:36) with *walking after the flesh;* **Chart 6**. (Galatians 5:19-21; Romans 6:16,21; 8:8; Luke 11:35)

18. If we have difficulty choosing to lay things down to God, what is the basic thing we must always keep in mind? (See Chapter Seven)

19. Many people today teach that our purpose as Christians is to "improve ourselves" and make us a "better us." Is this what the Bible teaches? (2 Corinthians 4:10-12; Galatians 2:20; Philippians 1:21) Explain.

20. How do we love God with all our will? (Deuteronomy 30:15-20; 1 Peter 4:2)

Personal Questions:

1. A choice that goes <u>against</u> what we naturally think, feel, and want is called a_____ _____. (Mark 9:24; Matthew 26:39; Luke 5:5c) Give examples in your own life where you had to make choices that you didn't feel, but because you were a willing and open vessel, God performed miracles through you in spite of how you felt.

2. Are there any situations in your life right now where you are having difficulty making *contrary choices* because of the circumstances, the other person's reactions, or your own emotions?

3. What three things happen when we make faith choices or contrary choices? God's Love becomes ___ _____; His Thoughts become ___ _____; and His Will becomes ___ _____.

4. The key to making contrary choices is simply to ___ _____. (Isaiah 1:19; Matthew 26:39; John 5:30b)

5. Maturity in Christ is simply:

(Hebrews 5:14; 2 Corinthians 4:10-12; Galatians 2:20)

6. Are there any other areas in your life right now where you may be able to apply this teaching?

7. Are there any key points in this chapter that you are still struggling with or having difficulty with? Explain.

Continue at Home:

1. Write on a note card all the Scriptures that ministered to you in this chapter. Use them to help you apply these principles. Memorize them.

2. Ask God to make you aware of your choices this week. Ask Him to remind you when you should be making contrary choices.

3. In Matthew 26:39 Jesus said, "Not my will, but thine." Write down some of your own thoughts and emotions that God has had you surrender to Him this week. (Ephesians 4:31; Colossians 3:5-9; Hebrews 12:15) Did you recognize them immediately? Did you give them over to God right away? Explain.

4. Philippians 2:13 says that God is in us not only "to will," but also "to do." This week, continually pray for His Power to produce His Life in you. (2 Corinthians 4:11-12) Share the situations He gives you to practice this.

READ:	MEMORIZE:
Romans 6 and 7	Mark 9:2
	1 John 5:20
	Philippians 2:13
	Matthew 26:39
	Luke 5:5

Chapter 13: Loving God With All Our Soul

Overview

Loving God with all our soul means *laying down our lives* so that God's Will can be performed through us. It's continually setting aside our lives in action, so that God's Life from our hearts can come forth and be manifested and shown forth through us.

We must not only make right faith choices, giving God the authority to work in us, but we must also give God our lives to perform those choices through. In other words, along with our faith choices, we must "present our bodies as living sacrifices." (Romans 12:1)

Loving God with all our soul means becoming one life with Him. It's exchanging our own image--all our thoughts, emotions and desires--for His Image--His Love, His Wisdom and His Power. This is the image we were created to bear from the very beginning.

"I am crucified with Christ: nevertheless I live; yet not I, but Christ liveth in me: and the life which I now live in the flesh I live by the faith (faithfulness) of the Son of God (to perform His Life through me)...." (Galatians 2:20)

The "faith we now live by" comes in the form of a choice, a faith choice to not only yield our wills to Him, but also to yield our souls and bodies to Him.

Group Discussion Questions: (Choose the most appropriate questions)

1. Describe the difference between our soul and our heart. (Proverbs 4:23; Isaiah 58:11)

2. Define our purpose as Christians. (1 John 4:7-8; Philippians 1:21; Ephesians 3:19; 2 Corinthians 4:10-11)

3. What determines whose life will be lived in our souls? (Isaiah 59:2)

4. We must do more than make the right *faith choice*. What other step of faith must we take in order for it to genuinely be God's Life flowing through us? (Romans 12:1; Galatians 5:25)

5. Loving God with all our soul means "exchanging our own self-image for the image we were created to bear, which is Christ's Image." Explain what this means. (Romans 8:29; 1 John 4:17; Colossians 3:10) Give some examples.

6. How is it that we are able to exchange our life for God's? (John 12:24-25; 1 Corinthians 15:31b; Matthew 26:39)

7. Define "identity." Give the four steps in building a healthy identity. (Isaiah 43:4; Luke 9:23-24; Philippians 1:21; 1 John 4:17)

8. Why does our confidence soar when we are "filled with God?" (2 Corinthians 3:5; 4:6-7) What happens when we refuse to allow God to conform us into His Image? (Ephesians 4:17-20; Romans 1:21-25,29; John 5:31)

9. Summarize what it is that causes us to have a poor self-image. (Jeremiah 5:25; Ezekiel 16:15; Romans 9:20; Matthew 23:25-27; Romans 7:15,19) Why does this occur even after we are Christians? (Isaiah 29:13; Romans 7:19-20) Give examples.

10. Name the three areas of our soul. Explain the "chain reaction" that occurs in our souls each time we choose to act.

11. Explain why are our thoughts are so important. Why must we learn to "take every thought captive"? (2 Corinthians 10:5-6; 2 Samuel 11:2-4)

12. Are we responsible for our initial negative (bad) thought? Why/Why not? What can we do the next time we have negative thoughts?

13. Is it wrong for a Christian to acknowledge his negative (bad) thoughts and feelings to himself and to God? Explain. What are the three ways we can "deal with" our negative thoughts and feelings as God would have us? What are we enabling Satan to do when we choose *not* to deal with these things? (Proverbs 5:22; John 8:34)

14. How can we tell the difference between God's voice, Satan's voice, and our own? What does the term "strongholds of the enemy" mean and why are these strongholds harder to get rid of? (Proverbs 5:22; John 8:34)

15. What happens when we "share" and "re-hash" our negative (bad) thoughts with others? (Ephesians 4:29-30; Isaiah 3:24a) What happens when we "dwell on" or try to "figure out" our past? What does God want us to do with our negative thoughts and past experiences? (Psalm 103:12; Galatians 5:24; Philippians 3:13b; Isaiah 43:18-19)

16. 2 Corinthians 10:3-6 talks about our "weapons of warfare." What are they and where is the battle waged?

17. When we realize we have "held on to" negative thoughts and emotions rather than release them to God, what are we to do? What is our responsibility? (Lamentations 3:41)

18. Describe why are our souls often compared to our "feet." (John 13:8-10)

19. Summarize some of the <u>results</u> we can expect when we lay down our wills and our lives to God. (Psalm 37:4-5; Luke 18:29-30; Matthew 6:31-33)

20. What does it mean to become *one Life* with God? (Philippians 1:20-21; 1 John 4:17; Deuteronomy 30:20; Galatians 2:20; Colossians 3:10) Why is it so critical to do this? (Isaiah 42:12; 1 Corinthians 10:31; 1 Peter 2:12; 4:11) Why is it so hard to do this in practice? (2 Corinthians 4:10a, 11a-12; John 12:24-26; Matthew 16:24; 23:26)

Personal Questions:

1. Our soul is a _____ area that can be filled with "God's Life," which is His _____, _____, and _____. (Colossians 1:27b; 1 John 4:8b) Or it can be filled with "self life," which is our own _____, _____, and _____. (John 5:31) What determines which "life" will be lived in our soul?

2. According to these Scriptures, what blessings do we receive from loving God with all our soul?

Luke 18:29-30

John 14:27

John 15:11

John 8:36 and 2 Corinthians 3:17

John 14:14

Romans 6:22-23

Romans 8:38-39

Galatians 5:22-23

Ephesians 1:18-19

James 1:12

3. Can you think of an example in your own life where you made the right faith choice, but forgot to lay down your life so God could perform His Will through you? What happened?

4. When you have difficulty laying down your life to God, what is the one basic fact you must always remember? (Isaiah 43:1-4; Matthew 10:29-31)

5. Is there anything in your life right now that you are afraid to lay down before God? If so, what is it and why are you afraid?

6. Consider if there is any area in your life right now where you have been trying to "improve yourself," rather than simply *exchanging lives* with God. Explain.

7. Has Satan ever brought up old thoughts and emotions that you thought you had already dealt with? If so, how did you handle them?

8. Why does God often allow negative feelings to remain even after we have made the right faith choices? Give examples.

9. Describe the areas in your life in which the enemy tries to ensnare or entrap you. (James 1:13-16) How can you resist these traps in the future?

10. Are you willing to constantly obey God's Word and trust His Spirit to perform His Will in your life? Are you willing to lay down your life and body, moment by moment, in order to be His instrument in this world? Pray and tell Him so.

Continue at Home:

1. Write on a note card all the Scriptures that particularly ministered to you in this chapter. Use them to help you apply these principles. Memorize them.

2. Ask God to show you any lies about yourself that you have programmed in over the years, and upon which you are basing your identity. Choose to give these over to God and replace them with His truth. (See the Who I Am in Christ Scriptures in the Supplemental Notes found in the textbook.)

3. Share a situation where you had no love for another person, and you had to be that "open vessel" so God could love them through you. What happened?

4. This week begin to "take every thought captive." Be aware of the chain reaction of your soul. Note examples and be ready to share.

5. Write down some of the results you see in yourself this week as you learn to love God as He desires. (Psalm 37:4-5; Luke 18:29-30; Matthew 6:31-33)

READ:	MEMORIZE:
John 13:7-10	Galatians 5:25
Colossians 1 and 3	Philippians 1:21
Ephesians 4	1 John 4:17
2 Corinthians 4	Mark 10:29-30

Chapter 14: Eight Steps to Survival

Overview

In Chapter 14 of the textbook we discuss eight steps that allow us to remain cleansed vessels, ready and willing for whatever God might call us to do. They are eight steps to maintaining our freedom of Spirit.

The first four steps are really formalities. These are not steps that we need to do each time we sin, but simply *attitudes* we need to have each day. The last four steps of the Survival Kit are *mandatory* steps and we must do these each time we have quenched God's Spirit in us (sinned).

Going through these four steps every time we are confronted with a hurtful remark, painful situation, pride, fear, doubt, anxiety, bitterness, resentment, etc., will keep us cleansed and prepared vessels for what God might want of us next.

These four steps were called the Inner Court ritual in the Old Testament. God gave these steps expressely to help His people deal their sin and be reconciled back to Him. And it's the same way with us.

"Let us draw near with a true heart in full assurance of faith, having our hearts sprinkled from an evil conscience, and our bodies washed with pure water." (Hebrews 10:22)

Group Discussion Questions:

1. What are the four *attitudes* we must constantly have in order to love the Lord in the way He desires? (Romans 12:1-2; Philippians 3:8-15; Philippians 2:5; 2 Corinthians 10:5-6) Do we need to "feel" each of these attitudes? Why/Why not? (Romans 1:17)

2. Romans 12:1 tells us we are to "present [our] bodies [as] a living sacrifice." What does this mean to you? (Job 13:15; 2 Corinthians 7:1; 2 Timothy 2:21)

3. When we talk about "denying ourselves," what exactly do we mean? (Philippians 3:8-15; John 12:24; Colossians 3:5,8-9) Are *all* Christians capable of denying themselves and "laying everything down?" If so, then why aren't more of us doing so?

4. Summarize why is it so important to "take every thought captive." (2 Corinthians 10:5-6) Is the first bad thought sin? Why/Why not? (2 Samuel 11:2-4)

5. What are the four *mandatory* steps (the Inner Court Ritual) that the Old Testament has laid out for us? (Proverbs 20:27; 2 Corinthians 13:5; Job 12:22; Proverbs 1:23; 1 John 1:9; Acts 8:22; Matthew 6:14-15; Colossians 3:5,8; Ephesians 5:26; John 15:3)

6. Why is it so important to ask God to expose the "root cause" of our thoughts and feelings? (Proverbs 5:22; Job 12:22) Why do we need to "see" these buried things? (Psalm 139:23-24)

7. Do the things we push down in our hidden chambers stay there, or do they affect our lives in some way? What do we enable Satan to do when we don't deal with these negative things? (Proverbs 5:22; John 8:34)

8. Define *confession* and *repentance*. (Isaiah 1:16; Ezekiel 18:30; 1 John 1:9)

9. If someone has offended us, do we wait to forgive him until he comes to us and asks? (Matthew 6:14-15; 18:32-35; Colossians 3:13) What if we are "justified" feeling the way we do?

10. In your own words, what does it mean to *give over to God* (sacrifice) all that He has shown us about ourselves? (Luke 11:39-40; 1 Peter 5:7; Ephesians 5:2; 2 Timothy 2:21) Give examples.

11. Who is responsible for changing our feelings? Can't we just pray hard and change our own feelings? Explain why or why not.

12. Why is it so important to "get into the Word" after we have given everything over (sacrificed) to the Lord? Explain. (Luke 11:24-26; Ephesians 5:26; John 15:3; James 1:21)

Personal Questions:

1. What do you "naturally" tend to do with your negative thoughts and feelings? (2 Corinthians 13:5) Give examples. What does God desire you to do? Are you willing? Write out the Inner Court Ritual for yourself.

2. Describe what specific self-centered thoughts, emotions, and desires get in your way of loving others with God's Agape Love. Write these down and then give them to God by going through the Inner Court Ritual.

3. Think of a person who triggers ungodly reactions in you. Pray and ask God to show you the *root cause* of these feelings. When God shows you, go through the Inner Court Ritual and give them to God. (Psalms 139:22-24)

4. Pray and ask God to show you other things you've been stuffing down in your hidden chambers. Deal with these things and, by faith, believe that God has cleansed you. Don't allow these things to come back by again thinking and meditating on them.

5. Why is it so important to have a consistent quiet time and to be in the Word daily? (2 Thessalonians 2:15; Proverbs 8:34-35; James 1:5-6; Matthew 7:24; Psalm 32:8; 119:105)

6. Write out five Scriptures that particularly ministered to you from this chapter and use them to help you apply these principles.

Continue at Home:

1. Start using the <u>Survival Kit Prayer</u> found in the back of Chapter 14. If this one does not suit you, write your own. Also write out on 3x5 cards the *mandatory steps* to take when God's Spirit is quenched. Keep these cards with you at all times. You will need them when you are away from your notebook and Bible.

2. Write a love letter to God and give Him all your hurts, anger, unforgiveness, etc. Go through the Inner Court Ritual. Remember He loves you and wants to wash all these things away by His blood. He wants to free you. Ask Him to reveal any areas of pride, unbelief, or other strongholds of the enemy. Allow Him to do so.

3. Ask God to make you more aware this week of any negative thoughts you might have toward others. Choose immediately to give these thoughts over to God (go through the four steps). Begin to make the Inner Court Ritual a *habit* in your life.

4. Simply be aware of anything that takes your peace away. Ask God to show you specifically what's quenching His Spirit and separating you. Note in your journal the things He tells you and the things you give over to Him. Note, also, the Scriptures He gives you to replace the lies and untruths.

READ:	MEMORIZE:
James 4	Psalm 119:9
Romans 6 and 7	1 John 1:9
Philippians 2 and 3	2 Corinthians 10:5

Chapter 15: Loving Others as Ourselves

Overview

1 Peter 1:22 sums up perfectly the three steps of loving God and also what we are to do now: "Seeing that ye have purified your souls in obeying the truth through the Spirit unto unfeigned love [Agape] of the brethren, [now] see to it that ye love [agapao] one another with a pure heart fervently."

Until we love God with all our heart, will and soul, loving others genuinely is impossible. There is no way we can totally give ourselves over to (and love) others, unless we have *first* totally given ourselves over to (and loved) God. God is the only One who can make loving others possible. However, once we have loved God, we can't stop there--we must go on and spread His Love to others.

When we love in the way God wants us to by loving others as ourselves, then all men will know--not by what we say but by how we live--that we are, indeed, Christians.

"By this shall all men know that ye are my disciples, *if ye have love one to another.*" (John 13:35, emphasis added)

Group Discussion Questions: (Choose the most appropriate questions)

1. In review, what does *agapao* mean? Who are we to love (agapao)? (1 Peter 1:22; 1 John 4:21; John 15:12-13; Matthew 22:37-39)

2. In Leviticus 19:18, God tells us to love one another. In the New Testament (John 13:34), however, Jesus calls "loving one another" a *new* commandment. Why is this now a new commandment?

3. How is it possible to love others *before or instead of* ourselves? (Matthew 22:37; 2 Corinthians 8:5: John 12:24; John 15:13; Philippians 2:5-9) Give examples.

4. John 13:34 tells us that Jesus is our example. How did Jesus love others? (John 15:9-17; 1 John 4:19; Matthew 20:28)

5. Why don't we see the Christian Body today loving like Jesus did? (Matthew 24:12) Why is God's Love growing cold in our hearts?

6. What is the most important way that others will know we are true Christians? (John 13:35; 1 John 3:10,14; 4:7-8,20) Give Scriptural examples.

7. Explain why we need to set our selves aside and become open vessels before we can love others as ourselves. (2 Corinthians 4:10-12; John 15:13; Philippians 2:5-9)

8. Is it "natural" for us to love in the way that God desires? (Ephesians 5:29; Isaiah 47:8)

9. Do we need to love ourselves first in order for us to love others? Why/Why not? (Ephesians 5:29; Philippians 2:21) Are we ever to love (agapao) ourselves? (Isaiah 47:8)

10. Describe the two primary ways we *naturally* love (are consumed with) ourselves. Give examples.

11. Why is there so much confusion in this area of "loving ourselves"? What is the root problem that God wants changed in each of us? (Philippians 2:21; Isaiah 47:8)

12. How does God desire His cycle of Love to work? (1 John 4:10-12; 3:16; John 17:26)

13. What gives us a healthy self-identity so we can go on and love God and others the way He desires? Explain the difference between *Christ-esteem and God-confidence* and self-esteem and self-confidence. (Isaiah 30:15; Proverbs 3:26; 14:26)

14. Name four practical ways we can love others. (1 John 3:18; 2 Corinthians 1:3-4; Philippians 2:3; Romans 14:13) Give examples.

15. Describe the secret to being real and genuine with others.

16. It's so difficult for us not to judge by appearance. What does Luke 16:15 have to say about this? Who is the only One to judge our hearts?

Personal Questions:

1. Loving others is only possible if we are _____ ____. (Matthew 22:37; 2 Corinthians 8:5) Then, God will enable us to love others ____ or _____ ___ ourselves. (2 Corinthians 4:10-12; 1 John 4:12)

2. Give an example of a situation where you experienced God's Love flowing through you. Did the situation change? Did the other person change? Were you able to continue to love even though you didn't see any changes? (1 Corinthians 13:8; Luke 6:27-28)

3. Only a person _____ _____ can be transparent and can admit failures about himself.

4. Self life wants to _____ __ _____, whereas God's Life wants to _____ __ _____.

5. Are there any key points in this chapter that you are still struggling with?

Continue at Home:

1. Write on a note card all the Scriptures in this chapter that particularly ministered to you. Use them to help you apply these principles. Memorize them.

2. Ask God to help you become aware of the times you are "consumed with yourself," either arrogantly or in a "self-pity" way. Choose to confess these things, repent of them, and give over to God. Go through your Inner Court Ritual.

3. If you feel you are not loving others the way God desires, ask Him to show you the areas in your life that are blocking your relationship with Him and preventing His Love from flowing.

4. This week as you learn more about loving others as yourself, ask God to show you further ways you can *agapao* your husband, your children, your parents, your family, your boss, etc. Begin to walk God's Love in your life. Be an *extension of His Love*.

READ:	MEMORIZE:
I John 3 and 4	1 Peter 1:22
John 14,15,17	1 John 4:7-8,12,17,21
1 Corinthians 13	John 15:12-13; 13:34
Hosea 1-3	1 John 3:18
Philippians 2	

Chapter 16: Loving in Our Marriages

Overview

The union that God seeks with us is illustrated metaphorically in the marriage union. God is the Lover and we are His chosen objects of Love. He courts us and draws us to Himself--waiting for our response. When we give ourselves to Him, He then pours His supernatural Love into our hearts through Jesus Christ. The marriage is then "consummated" and sealed with the indwelling of the Holy Spirit. The Groom has become "one" with His bride.

God designed human marriage to be a prophetic picture of our love relationship with Him. He wanted us to have an earthly picture of how wonderful our love union with Him could be. How grieved He must be with what we have done with His model.

God's Will for our lives as husbands and wives is, as God designed, to unconditionally love each other no matter what. Therefore, if we are not loving (agapao) our spouses "as ourselves," then there is really something wrong with our relationship with God and we are not loving Him as we should.

"If a man say, I love God, and hateth his brother, he is a liar; for he that loveth not his brother, whom he hath seen, how can he love God, whom he hath not seen?" (1 John 4:20)

We must be willing to love our spouse with God's Love even if our circumstances and our situations never change. Our motivation is wrong if we are loving only to have the circumstances or the other person change. That's human love and not God's Love at all. Even if the result of our loving unconditionally is totally opposite to what we would like to see, as long as we are loving God's way, He promises us His *Agape will never fail.*

Group Discussion Questions: (Choose the most appropriate questions)

1. Whether we are married, separated, divorced, single, or widowed, what is the most important thing we can do? (1 Peter 4:8; 1 John 3:17-18; 4:7-8,20-21; John 13:35; Romans 13:8)

2. If we are not loving with God's Love, what is wrong? (1 John 3:14-15; 4:7-8,20) Why?

3. In Ephesians 5:22 it says, "Wives, submit yourselves unto your own husbands." If we have a hard time with this principle, what Scripture should we remember to apply first?

4. If we still cannot lay our wills and our lives down to our spouses because of "justified hurts," what further Scriptures should we always keep in mind?

5. Who loved (agapao) us, even when we were still enemies of the cross? (Romans 5:8; 19-21)

6. What is it that teaches us how to love wisely? (Psalm 32:8)

7. Define "sloppy Agape" or unbalanced love.

8. When we encounter someone in our family emersed in sin, in general, what is the best way to handle it? (1 Peter 4:8) Do we point out the sin to them and try to fix it ourselves? (Colossians 3:12-13; Hosea 1-3; Romans 2:4; 12:21)

9. What are our own three responsibilities in loving our spouses? (Isaiah 43:4a; Matthew 22:37; Matthew 22:39) What are God's responsibilities in our marriages? (James 1:5; Psalm 32;8; Romans 8:28; Isaiah 55:8-9)

10. If our spouse asks us to do something ungodly, what should our response be? (Exodus 1:17; Daniel 3 & 6; Acts 5:29)

11. Think of some Scriptural examples where God's Love and His Wisdom were the complete solution to the problems. (Hosea 1-3; Genesis 37:5-45:8) Are there any circumstances or situations in your life where God's Love can't be the solution? (John 13:35; 1 Corinthians 13:8a)

12. Should we "stop loving" if our spouses or our circumstances never change? (1 Corinthians 13:4-8; Romans 5:3-5; 1 John 4:7-8, 20-21; Luke 6:27-28) Why/Why not?

13. What basic principle of the gospel has been forgotten in many of our Christian marriages and homes today? (Galatians 2:20; 5:24; 2 Corinthians 4:10)

14. In conclusion, summarize *God's Way of Agape.* (Matthew 22:37-39; Matthew 16:24-25; John 12:24; 2 Corinthians 4:10-12)

Personal Questions:

1. The definition of marriage is a commitment or a _____ before the Lord. (Deuteronomy 23:21; Ecclesiastes 5:4) Marriage in God's eyes means to fit, join, and _____ ____. (Genesis 2:23-24; 1 Peter 3:8; Philippians 2:2; 1 Corinthians 1:10; Matthew 19:5-6; Ephesians 5:28)

2. Why did God institute marriage in the first place? (Hosea 2:20)

3. In any marriage, God's_____ and His _____ must always work together. (Ephesians 3:17-19; 4:15a; Philippians 1:9) Why?

4. Which type of love (human or divine) best describes your marriage? Explain.

5. READ: Genesis 12:11-20 and 1 Peter 3:5-6. Who can we trust to deal with our spouse's sin? Explain. (John 8:3-12; Romans 2:4; 1 Peter 3:1-2; 2 Samuel 7:14; Hebrews 12:5-7) Give Scriptural examples.

6. Our two basic needs are __ __ _____ and __ _____. Is it our spouses' responsibility to meet these two needs for us? Why/Why not? (Philippians 4:19)

7. Are you "living the truth" in your home--do your words and your deeds match? In other words, do your actions inside your home match your words at church? Can your spouse tell that you are a Christian by your actions?

8. See the *Marriage Relationship* Scriptures in the Supplemental Notes found in the back of the textbook. Put the ones that particularly minister to you on 3x5 cards and memorize them.

9. John 10:10 says that God desires us to have *abundant Life* right where we are walking today. Are you experiencing this? Explain.

10. The meaning to life lies in our _____. First our _____ with God and then our _____ with others. (Luke 10:25,27-28) Joy, peace, and love come not with the absence of _____, but only with the presence of _____. (Psalm 16:11; 1 John 4:7-8)

Continue for the Rest of Your Life:

Don't put this study on a shelf and forget it. Continually keep God's
Way of Agape foremost in your mind. Keep reading The Way of Agape
textbook and listening to the tapes. Constantly renew your thinking in
order to stay an open channel, receiving His Love, and then being a vessel to
pass it on.

"If ye, then, be risen with Christ, seek those things which are above,
where Christ sitteth on the right hand of God. Set your affection on things
above, not on things on the earth. For ye are dead, and your life is hidden
with Christ in God. When Christ, *who is our life*, shall appear, then shall ye
also appear with Him in glory.

"Mortify, therefore, your members which are upon the earth...put off all
these: anger, wrath, malice, blasphemy, filthy communication out of your
mouth. Lie not one to another, seeing that ye have put off the old man with
his deeds, And have put on the new man, which is renewed in knowledge
after the image of Him that created him....*And above all these things put on
[Agape],* which is the bond of perfectness." (Colossians 3:1-5, 8-10, 14)

Conclusion

God is Love and, if we are believers, His Love is "in us" (in our hearts). The only way, however, that His Love can come forth from our hearts out into our lives is if we are open and cleansed vessels. We must constantly choose to set aside, relinquish, and die to our own self (our own thoughts, emotions, and desires that are contrary to God's) so that God can love His Love through us.

The reason God so often allows trials and tribulations into our lives is so we might learn to unconditionally lay down at His feet all our thoughts, emotions, and desires that are contrary to His, justified or not. Then His Love in our hearts will not "grow cold," as Matthew 24:12 warns, but will freely flow out into all our relationships. And we can "be in this world as He is," and that is *LOVE*!

"Strait is the gate, and narrow is the way, which leadeth unto life, and *few* there be that find it." (Matthew 7:14, emphasis added)

Will you be one that does?

Role of the Discussion Leader

Your role as a leader is simply to stimulate discussion by asking the appropriate questions and encouraging people to respond.

Your leadership is a gift to the other members of the group. Keep in mind that they, too, share responsibility for the group. If you are nervous, realize you are not the first to feel this way. Many Biblical leaders--Moses, Joshua, and even the apostle Paul--felt nervous and inadequate to lead others.

Leader Objectives

The following are suggested objectives to help you become an effective leader.

- To guide the discussion, to clarify understanding, and to keep the group focused on the lesson.

- To steer the group into a meaningful exchange among themselves.

- To help the participants learn from each other.

- To keep the group discussion focused on the key points found in the Scriptural Reference Outlines at the end of each chapter.

- To be a neutral person leading the discussion back to Scripture and the key points if it wanders.

- To assist the group in finding practical applications for the principles discussed.

- To encourage each person to participate in the group discussion.

- To make the discussion group a non-threatening place for all to share their ideas.

- To have a positive attitude and to provide encouragement to the group.

- To guide, rather than dominate, the discussion.

Preparing to Lead

First of all, it's critical that you, the leader of the discussion group, be a cleansed vessel filled with God's Love and Wisdom--a "living example" of God's Way of Agape. This message must first be applied to your own life. Otherwise, you will not be genuinely prepared to lead others. You must have a working knowledge of the Way of Agape principles, so you can share what God has done in your own life. You cannot "give out" something you have never "experienced" for yourself.

Only by being real and transparent yourself, sharing your own failures as well as your victories, will genuineness ever be brought into the discussion. It's important to remember that you *don't have to be "perfect" in order to guide a discussion, you simply must be an open vessel pointing others to the only One who is perfect--and that's Jesus.*

Paramount to any Bible study is prayer. Be sure to pray for the group before and after each study and do much private prayer during the discussion itself. Pray for each member of the group during the week, always remembering that prayer is the only thing that unleashes the power of God to work in all our lives.

Read the assigned chapter in The Way of Agape textbook. Answer each question in the corresponding chapter in the workbook. Meditate and reflect upon each passage of Scripture as you formulate your answers.

Familiarize yourself with the Scriptural Reference Outlines at the end of each chapter in the textbook. These will help you understand the important points to make in the discussion and provide more information about the questions.

You might also want to purchase The Way of Agape Leader's Guide containing "suggested" answers for each question. There are no "right" answers; these are just suggestions. Be sure to allow the Holy Spirit room to answer the questions the way He desires.

As a leader, you must be a sensitive listener, not only to the members of the group but also to the Holy Spirit. As you ask the appropriate questions, allow the Holy Spirit to direct your responses and give you discernment as to who needs a special touch (a hug, an encouragement, time afterwards, etc.).

Remember, as the leader of the discussion, you are simply a channel God is using to stimulate and guide the conversation--the Holy Spirit is always the teacher. Do not do all the talking, but involve every member of the group, always seeing that the sharing is edifying and pointed towards Jesus.

Leading the Study

Always begin the study on time. If everyone realizes that you begin on time, the members of the group will make a greater effort to be there on time--they won't want to miss anything.

At the beginning of your first meeting, you might share that these studies are designed to be discussions, not lectures. Encourage everyone to participate.

The discussion questions in the workbook are designed to be used just as they are written. If you wish, you may read each one aloud to the group. Or you may prefer to express them in your own words. However, unnecessary rewording of the questions is not recommended.

Don't be afraid of silence. People in the group need time to think before responding.

Try to avoid answering your own questions. If necessary, keep rephrasing a question until it is clearly understood. If the group thinks you will always answer for them, they will keep silent.

Encourage more than one answer to each question. You might ask, "What do the rest of you think?" or "Anyone else?" Allow several people to respond.

Never reject an answer. Be as affirming as possible. If a person's answer is clearly wrong, you might ask, "What lead you to that conclusion?" Or let the group handle the problem by asking them what they think about the question.

Avoid going off on tangents. If people wander off course, gently bring them back to the question at hand.

Try to end on time. This is often difficult to do, but if you control the pace of the discussion by not spending too much time on some questions, you should be able to finish at the appropriate time. A discussion group of about 45 minutes to an hour is perfect.

Additional Suggestions for Leaders

Besides being that open and cleansed vessel and constantly praying, there are several other *skills* that you, as the leader of the discussion, should pray about developing:

Pray for and develop *good communication skills.* Communication will not only be your words, but also your "body language." Even though someone might share something shocking in the discussion, be careful not to offend the participant by your response. Acknowledge the person, yet all the while asking God for *His* response to what they have just shared. Be confident that God will give you the Love you need and also the Wisdom you need to respond "wisely in Love."

Try to really understand what the participant is sharing. If necessary, repeat what you think he/she is saying. For example, you might ask: "Is this what you are saying..." or, "You mean...?"

Another very important asset for you, as the leader of the group, to acquire is to be a *good listener.* Everyone is desperate for someone to listen to them, especially when they are going through critical emotional issues. Whenever someone is talking, give them your undivided attention. Your eyes should be on the person sharing and you should try to acknowledge them as much as you can (again, always praying silently to God for His response).

Another vital skill to develop is to *be an encourager.* Set an example for your group by encouraging the members continually. Without encouragement, your sharing times will be nothing more than answering homework questions at school. (You might even suggest that the following week, each of the members of the group phone and encourage someone else in the group.)

One of the most difficult tasks that you will face is *how to keep one person from dominating* the group. You need to allow each person in the group an opportunity to share, but you must prevent any *one* person from doing all the talking (including yourself). One member of the group who continually dominates the discussion can derail and quench an otherwise anointed sharing time. You mustn't rush the person speaking, giving the Holy Spirit ample time to minister and guide the discussion, but at the same time you are responsible to keep the discussion on target and to accomplish all that needs to be done.

A few suggestions to prevent one person dominating the discussion:

● You might interrupt the particular person speaking and restate what you have just heard him/her say.

● You might repeat the question you previously asked the group. The dominating person might be startled at first by the interruption, but should respond by answering the second question more directly.

● If this does not work, then you should ask the participant to please let the other group members share their views also.

Another invaluable skill for you, as the leader of the discussion, to have is knowing how to *involve all the members* of the group in the discussion. Discussion groups are not for lecturing--each individual must be encouraged to interact. Ideally, everyone should have an opportunity to share. Ask open-ended questions to specific individuals, especially ones that are reluctant to volunteer anything themselves.

Again, it's important not to criticize, make fun of, or put anyone down. Remember, be an encourager. Learn how to correct a group member's answer in a positive way and then, as tactfully as you can, go on to the next person.

Helpful Hints for Leaders

Always open the discussion with prayer and close the session with prayer. Pray that God will help each of you to apply the Biblical principles daily.

Start out the first session by sharing a little about yourself. How has the Way of Agape affected or changed your life? Go around the circle and have each member share five minutes about him/herself.

In the succeeding meetings, begin each session by asking:

• "Which key points stood out to you during this session?"

• "Which points challenged you or encouraged you?"

• "Could any of you relate to some of the situations or struggles that were shared in this chapter?

• "Are any of you experiencing similiar situations?"

• "In what areas of your life might you be able to apply this teaching?"

Suggest that each member of the group during the week write down any questions they may have while reading the textbook, listening to the tapes or watching the video, so they can talk about them during the group discussion.

Lean heavily on the Scriptural Reference Outlines at the end of each chapter for the *key points* to emphasize.

Reproduce **Charts 1-6** in Chapter 10 of The Way of Agape textbook and post them in each of the appropriate sessions, so the group can constantly refer to them.

Finally, stress complete confidentiality. Set an example for the group by being the first to be trustworthy.

"Blessed be God, even the Father of our Lord Jesus Christ, the Father of mercies, and the God of all comfort; Who comforteth us in all our tribulation, that we may be able to comfort them which are in any trouble, by the comfort wherewith we ourselves are comforted of God."

2 Corinthians 1:3-4